I0814941

GREAT SPORTS RIVALRIES

THE MICHIGAN WOLVERINES

Jamie Fickett

THE OHIO STATE BUCKEYES

A Stingray Book

Teaching Tips for Caregivers and Teachers:

This Hi-Lo book features high-interest subject matter that will appeal to all readers in intermediate and middle school grades. It may be enjoyed by students reading at or above grade level as well as by those who are looking for age-appropriate themes matched with a less challenging reading level. Hi-Lo books are ideal for ELL readers, too.

Each book appeals to a striving reader's age and maturity level. Opportunities are provided for students to read words they already know while encountering a limited number of new, high-interest vocabulary words. With these supports in place, students will read more fluently while increasing reading comprehension. Use the following suggestions to help students grow as readers.

- Encourage the student to read independently at home.
- Encourage the student to practice reading aloud.
- Encourage activities that require reading.
- Establish a regular reading time.
- Have the student write questions about what they read.

Teaching Tips for Teachers:

Before Reading

- Ask, "What do I know about this topic?"
- Ask, "What do I want to learn about this topic?"

During Reading

- Ask, "What is the author trying to teach me?"
- Ask, "How is this like something I already know?"

After Reading

- Discuss how the text features (headings, index, etc.) help with understanding the topic.
- Ask, "What interesting or fun fact did you learn?"

TABLE OF CONTENTS

BIG TEN BATTLERS

The **rivalry** between the Michigan Wolverines and the Ohio State Buckeyes is one of the best in college sports. Both NCAA (National Collegiate Athletic Association) teams play in the Big Ten Conference.

The big November game between the football rivals is always the last one on each team's regular schedule.

The teams have met at least 117 times. Of those games, Michigan won 60, and Ohio State won 51. Six games were ties.

FUN FACT

The University of Michigan is in Ann Arbor, Michigan. The Ohio State University is in Columbus, Ohio.

6
B1G
6
26
B1G
26

1897: THE RIVALRY BEGINS

The first matchup between the teams was in 1897. The Wolverines won 34 to 0.

Michigan dominated in the early years. Although the teams played nearly every year, Ohio State did not win until 1919.

The rivals were more equally matched in the 1920s through the 1940s. Competition heated up, and there were many wins and losses on both sides.

FUN FACT

Tensions between Ohio and Michigan began in the early 1800s, when both states claimed a piece of land at their border. Ohio got the land. Michigan got the Upper Peninsula.

1950: THE SNOW BOWL

Ohio State and Michigan played for the Big Ten Championship on November 25, 1950.

The temperature was a freezing 10 degrees Fahrenheit (-12 degrees Celsius). Winds blew at 28 miles (45 kilometers) per hour. Heavy snow was falling.

The teams battled it out as the snow piled up. Michigan won 9 to 3 with only 27 yards of **offense**.

The game came to be known as the "Snow Bowl."

74
71
52
52

1969: THE TEN-YEAR WAR BEGINS

Bo Schembechler

In 1969, Ohio State was ranked first in the country. Under head coach Woody Hayes, the Buckeyes had won every game in their season by at least 27 points.

The Wolverines had a new head coach, Bo Schembechler.

The teams played on November 22, 1969. It was an **upset**. Michigan won 24 to 12.

The game began an intense competition between Coach Hayes and Coach Schembechler. It came to be known as the "Ten-Year War."

FUN FACT

Bo Schembechler was an Ohio State assistant coach under Woody Hayes before he went to Michigan.

1972 and 1973: WAR YEARS

In 1972, Ohio State was led by an impressive freshman running back, Archie Griffin. Michigan had an outstanding defense. Michigan lost 11 to 14.

In 1973, the game ended in a tie. The teams would share the Big Ten Championship. This created a problem. The winning team usually went to the Rose Bowl.

Big Ten leaders held a vote. They decided to send Ohio State to the Rose Bowl since Michigan's quarterback had a shoulder injury.

FUN FACT

Archie Griffin is the only college player to win two Heisman Trophies.

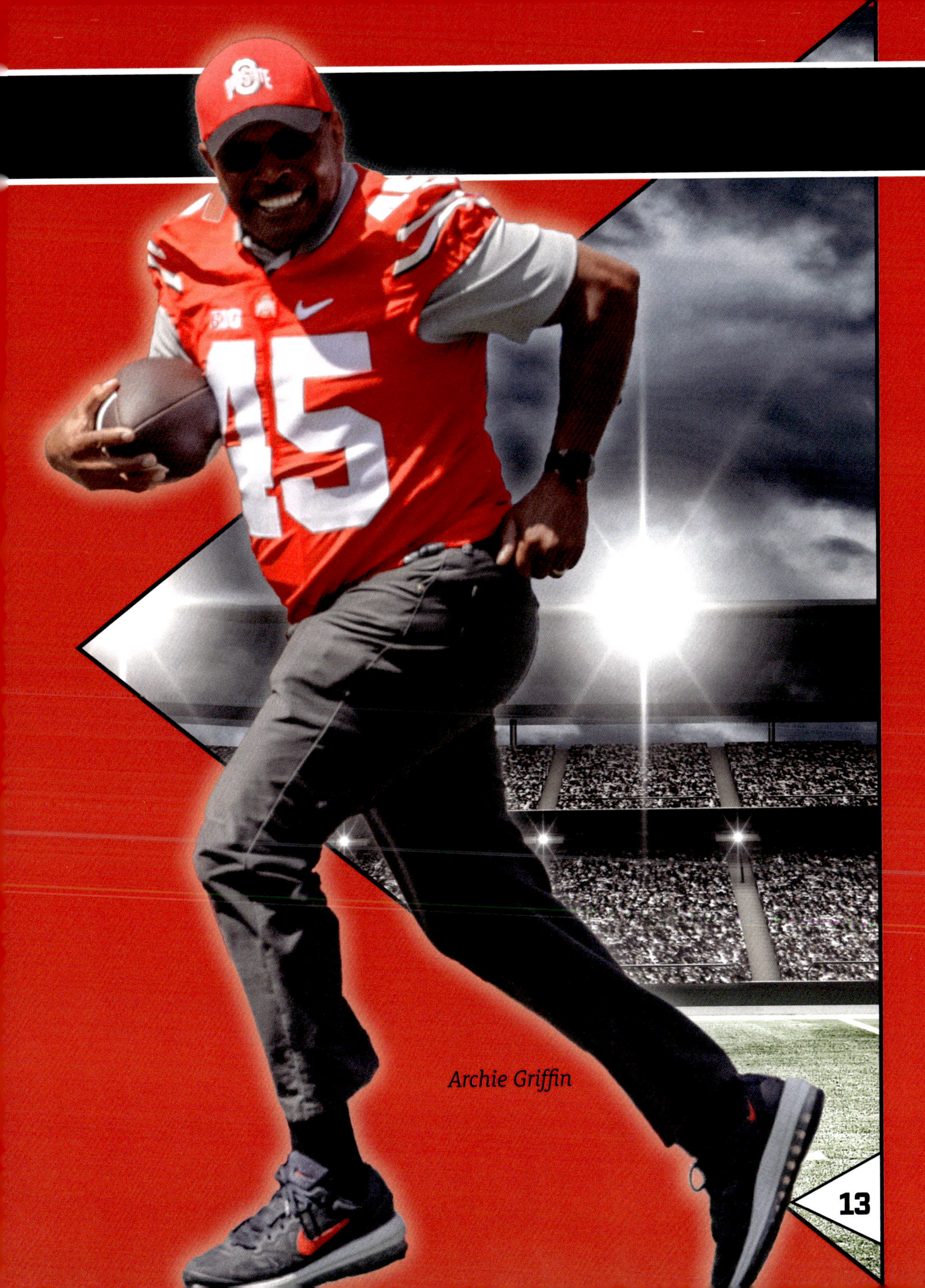
Archie Griffin

1970s: MORE WAR YEARS

In 1974, the Michigan kicker missed a **field goal** in the final seconds. Ohio State won 12 to 10.

In 1975, the teams were tied 14 to 14 in the fourth quarter. The Buckeye defense **intercepted** a pass, leading to an Ohio State touchdown. The Buckeyes won 21 to 14.

Michigan dominated in 1976, winning 22 to 0.

In the final minutes of the 1977 game, Ohio State was in position to score. But they fumbled the ball. The Wolverines won 14 to 6.

FUN FACT

The Ten-Year War lasted from 1969 to 1978. The teams played 10 games. Michigan won five. Ohio State won four. One game was a tie.

1990s: WOLVERINE WONDER

Michigan had lots of success against Ohio State in the 1990s.

In 1990, offensive star Desmond Howard helped the Wolverines win with five catches for 73 yards and a touchdown.

Michigan went on to **rout** Ohio State 31 to 3 in 1991. Howard had a 93-yard punt return for a touchdown.

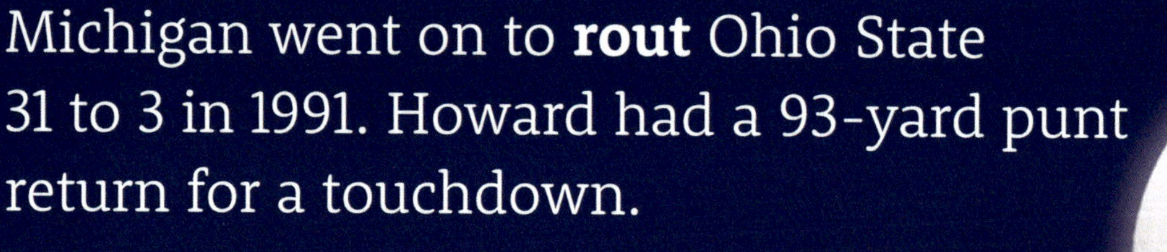

FUN FACT

Desmond Howard is a host of the pregame show **College GameDay.**

FREEMAN
1

2000s: BUCKEYES IN CONTROL

From 2000 to 2019, Ohio State ruled the rivalry. The Wolverines beat the Buckeyes just three times.

In 2016, the teams were ranked second and third in the nation. Michigan had star safeties Jabrill Peppers and Dymonte Thomas. Ohio State was led by quarterback J.T. Barrett and wide receiver Curtis Samuel.

In double overtime, on fourth down, Barrett made a **controversial** first down. Samuel raced into the end zone for an Ohio State win.

FUN FACT

Ohio State coaches Jim Tressel and Urban Meyer each won six games in a row against Michigan.

THE RIVALRY CONTINUES

Today's star players continue the **epic** rivalry between the Michigan Wolverines and the Ohio State Buckeyes.

Each year, these schools **recruit** some of the best players in the country.

Who will win the next battle between these two great teams?

FUN FACT

With two interceptions, Michigan beat Ohio State in 2023. The Wolverines went on to win the National Championship.

OHIO STATE
OHIO STATE

GLOSSARY

controversial (kahn-truh-VUR-shuhl): causing a great deal of disagreement

epic (EP-ik): amazing or impressive

field goal (feeld gohl): a play in which the ball is kicked from the field, through the goalposts, scoring three points

intercepted (in-tur-SEP-tid): caught a ball that was passed by the other team

offense (AW-fens): yards gained when a team moves the ball down the field toward the opponent's end zone

recruit (ri-KROOT): to convince a player to join your team; coaches recruit athletes

rivalry (RYE-vuhl-ree): a longstanding, competitive, up-and-down relationship between two teams

rout (rout): to totally defeat

upset (uhp-SET): an unexpected defeat

INDEX

AFTER READING QUESTIONS

1. Which team has won more games against the other?
2. How did the Wolverines win the game in 1977?
3. Why was the game on November 25, 1950, called the Snow Bowl?
4. What was the Ten-Year War?
5. What required a vote in 1973?

ABOUT THE AUTHOR

Jamie Fickett lives in Long Island, New York. He enjoys sports, especially baseball. He likes to go to Mets games to watch his favorite player, Pete Alonso, play. He also enjoys cooking his famous chili and watching Formula 1 racing.

Written by: Jamie Fickett
Design by: Kathy Walsh
Editor: Kim Thompson

Library of Congress PCN Data
The Michigan Wolverines vs. The Ohio State Buckeyes
/Jamie Fickett
Great Sports Rivalries
ISBN 979-8-8873-5949-6 (hard cover)
ISBN 979-8-8873-5988-5 (paperback)
ISBN 979-8-8904-2047-3 (EPUB)
ISBN 979-8-8904-2106-7 (eBook)
Library of Congress Control Number: 2023912510

Printed in the United States of America.

Photographs/Shutterstock/Newscom: Cover: Jose/Marinmedia.Org/CsmviaNewscom, Zac BonDurant/Icon SportswireviaNewscom; p 5, 6, 9, 10, 13, 14, 17, 18, 21: EFKS; p 6: Scott Terna; p 8: Lon Horwedel/Icon Sportswire; p 10: Zack MeiselviaNewscom; p 13: Scott Stuart via Newscom; p 14: Steven King/Icon Sportswire; p 17: Scott Terna/Cal Sport Media; p 18: Scott Stuart; p 21: Aaron Josefczyk

Seahorse Publishing Company
www.seahorsepub.com

Published in the United States
Seahorse Publishing
PO Box 771325
Coral Springs, FL 33077